Finding the Way Home

By

Fabiola Sully

ISBN: 0-7596-5363-1

This book is printed on acid free paper.

1stBooks – rev. 01/03/02

The Rock

The rock has been through hell.

It has been through huge blizzards.

It has been through thunderstorms.

It has been through hurricanes.

And being kicked by many people.

But do you want to know something else?

No matter how much pain it takes.

It still manages to stand.

Fabiola Sully

Who Am I

I'm the one you tease

Cause I'm different.

I'm the one you bother

Cause I'm just there.

I'm the mat you step on.

I'm the rock you kick around.

And you think you can control me.

Like I'm the clay and you're the sculptor.

Like I'm the robot and you press my buttons.

But you can't control me.

I may be nothing as you say.

But your words don't mean jack to me.

Fabiola Sully

I am somebody.

Sooner or later you'll see me on the street.

With my head up high.

While you're eating my dust.

And I'll be wondering,

Who's laughing now!

Fabiola Sully

Beauty

Can you tell a lot a person?

By just their beauty

Can you tell what they like?

Or how they think?

Can you tell what life is to them

By their sparkling eyes,

And flawless skin

Do you know if they like midnight walks?

Do you know if they like sports?

Or even like it rough when making love.

But most of all,

Fabiola Sully

Do you know who they really are?

And will love you back.

Because it can be a distraction.

To what lies ahead.

So beware and keep guard.

Before it sucks you in.

Fabiola Sully

This Day

I never thought

This day will come.

When I feel more alive

And I could say I survived.

I got the strength to get out of bed.

And look out my window.

The sun was shining on my face.

As I grinned,

Relinquishing the darkness,

That had spread through my room.

I watched the trees and the birds.

The people walking by,

Fabiola Sully

The children playing,

And I knew I wasn't an outsider anymore.

I never thought this day would come.

When I could open my eyes.

See clearly what is in front of me.

The beginning of my new life.

Fabiola Sully

Sitting on the Park Bench

I was sitting in the park one summer day.

Taking notices to nature and people around me.

I watched a little boy climbing the monkey bars.

While his mother watched in concern.

But she didn't hold on to him.

She grew a smile as he climbed higher.

I took notice of a couple arguing.

Tears wear rolling down her face.

As her boyfriend walked away.

She stood there motionless.

And smiled with her watery eyes.

I watched an elderly couple walking pass me.

They walked with canes and seemed crippled.

Fabiola Sully

But they were laughing and carrying on.

I can't control what is going on around me.

But I can never let that interfere.

From me being happy.

Fabiola Sully

Saying I'm Sorry

So here we are,

Eye to eye.

Still far apart,

Neither of us moves an inch.

We don't lose our edge.

Neither one of us says anything.

The other will smell the weakness.

We still care for each other.

But things have to be said.

You have your pride,

I have mine.

Fabiola Sully

We're not giving that up easily.

So we stand here,

Looking at each other.

While the pain grows in our hearts.

Fabiola Sully

Perceptions

You say to me,

That I have beauty that stands out.

My hair's thick and straight.

My skin's pale and flawless,

And my eyes are very distinctive.

I should be a model,

Or even better, on a pedestal.

But what would you say,

If I told you I wasn't prefect.

That I have split ends.

That I get pimples on my face.

Or cuts and rashes on my skin

Or what would you say.

Fabiola Sully

If I told you that I'm black.

Would you still put me up there?

You think I'm pulling your leg.

Maybe next time

You see the whole me.

Rather than selected parts.

Fabiola Sully

The Gift

I give you this gift,

To show how much you mean to me.

It's not something I could wrap.

Or put in a box.

But there's a catch to this gift.

You must handle it with care.

Treasure it like it is your own.

And remember who gave it to you.

Cause it cost me a lot,

And I can't get a refund back from it.

Fabiola Sully

Temptations

When I saw you standing there

With that mischievous grin on your face.

I knew there was trouble ahead.

I remember the way you used to touch me.

I remember the way you used to kiss.

But I am strong.

I can handle you.

But the more I look at you,

The more I want you.

It is too risky for me,

But I am weakening.

Fabiola Sully

I want to walk away,

But my feet aren't moving.

You kiss me with your tender lips.

I'm caught again.

Fabiola Sully

Faby's song (prayer to God)

I've been sitting in my room.

Looking over my life.

Reexaming myself,

Trying to find myself.

I thought I had everything together.

But still managed to break down.

I was given whatever I wanted,

But can't crack a smile.

I want to be loved,

But my heart is stone cold to receive it.

I need to take risks in life.

But I don't have the guts to go forward.

Fabiola Sully

Everybody knows my name.

But people still don't know me.

The world is going faster.

And I am being left behind.

I know I deserve more.

Than what I have been given.

I feel like I have failed you.

But I feel you have faith in me.

And know what I am worth.

So I'll just keep on moving and my head up.

Searching for my purpose.

And when my time comes,

I will feel worthy of what you have given me.

Fabiola Sully

Pretty Brown eyes

He has a certain look,

That would make his mama proud.

He has a smile

That would light up a room.

He has a deep voice

That would make a woman melt.

He wore gold all over,

That would blind you.

And his eyes,

His soft brown eyes shines through the light.

But look through them carefully.

They may be pretty,

Fabiola Sully

But they're telling you something.

He's not what you thought he would be.

So turn around,

Don't look back.

He may be a dream.

But his pretty brown eyes,

Will put you back to reality.

Fabiola Sully

The Road

The scattered glass pieces,

The used old needles

Around to hurt me

The papers and garbage,

The cracks and mold

Making it less attractive.

All covered with thick smoke,

And toxic waste everywhere.

Sending shivers down my spine.

I felt a light-headed as I walked.

With the smell of vomit and filth in my path.

I don't know where I'm heading.

Fabiola Sully

I don't know how long it will take me.

But I feel I will accomplish something.

That will change my life.

When I reach the end.

Fabiola Sully

Maritza

I looked through your brown eyes,

With your content grin

Wondering where has this girl

With the inquisitive mind had gone.

Yesterday, you were a baby,

Following me wherever I went,

And never wanted to be lonely.

But now you have become independent.

You don't cling on me,

Or ask your cute questions.

As I watched you grow,

I still feel that you need me.

Fabiola Sully

I would shield you from the pain and drama,

The suffering and hate

I have experienced in this world.

That's if life would let me.

But I understand you need to grow,

And I don't want to be blamed,

For holding you back.

So I must set you free

For you to see what life has to offer you.

But in the back of my mind,

You're still the baby who clings on me.

Fabiola Sully

Diamond in the Rough

You were brought into this world

By god almighty,

But you must face many situations,

Through your beautiful life.

You're too fat; you're too skinny.

You're hair is nappy; you're breasts are too small

You're too dark; you're too high strung.

You'll never go through life.

Looking the way you are.

But that's all they're thinking.

They don't know any better.

I understand how painful it gets.

Fabiola Sully

I have been on this road before.

Always doubting myself and my looks,

And taking in everything people have said to me.

Be proud of yourself.

Accept the fact that you are different.

Walk away from the insults and comments made by people.

Who are insecure about themselves.

You may have to work harder

To gain your respect

And always remember,

God doesn't make mistakes.

Fabiola Sully

Bag Lady

I watched this lady hop on the bus.

Who looked about my age.

With two bags on each hand.

Struggling to get on board,

And taking her money out.

Trying to find somewhere to sit,

As she bumped into people.

Everybody was staring at her,

Like she was a sideshow.

Giving her dirty looks,

And laughing as she passed by.

No one did seem to help her.

Fabiola Sully

Even with struggle written on her face.

When her stop came,

She hurdled he way to the front of the bus.

She got off buy a clothing store,

And just stood there,

Looking at her reflection in the store window.

I watched her as she walked away.

Leaving her bags on the curb.

Not even turning back.

I know she didn't see me.

But I clapped for her as she walked away.

For I use to be her.

Fabiola Sully

Just Like You

I have been degraded by society

Cause of what I am.

I have to work at everything I do

Cause I'm not taken seriously.

I have been labeled

Cause they are too ignorant to know me.

I have to be stubborn

Cause the nice game doesn't work for me.

I have to be cautious

Cause nothing is a free ride.

So remember this, my friend,

Fabiola Sully

I may be pale-skinned,

But I have obstacles

Just like you.

Fabiola Sully

The Other Side

Please don't send me to the other side.

You wouldn't like me if you did.

I'll morph into another being.

My eyes will flare.

My skin will boil.

I'll roar like the Leo,

While shooting of words of the devil

Losing control,

Of my body and psyche.

Trying to struggle

To get into neutral

So please don't send me to the other side.

You wouldn't like me if you did.

Fabiola Sully

The Mirror

I remember when you use to look at me.

With pride in your eyes,

You were proud of your full-figured hips,

Your breasts, and your face.

You loved yourself so much.

But you are changing.

And I have lost respect for you.

You changed your hair color,

You changed your attitude.

You never even smile.

All you do is cry when you look at me.

You want to be somebody else.

Fabiola Sully

Someone you think is worthy.

Well, I think you are a punk.

I think you lost sight of yourself and your dreams.

You think you're hot stuff.

But you're only destroying yourself.

I know the truth.

I know who you really are.

I'll wake you up when you really see me!

Fabiola Sully

My Candy Bar

My candy bar,

No nuts, no raisins.

Can be milk chocolate

Or just plain dark.

I get a little temptation

Every time I see it.

I open the wrapper,

And look at it with passion.

I take a bite out of it.

Not even chewing,

Just letting the taste fills my mouth,

And entice every part of my body.

Fabiola Sully

But sometimes it's not good to have it all at once.

So I put it back in the wrapper.

And save it for later

My candy bar

Fabiola Sully

By Your Side

I believe faith bought us her,

In each other's arms.

And faith already had a notion.

That we were different.

I feel the restraints and the bumps,

The moodiness, the gripes

And the tension I have sense,

Through this path of love.

I feel our love is a river

Not expecting the high tides

Or when the weather will change.

Or when the water calms down.

Fabiola Sully

We push each other away,

But still feel needed by each other.

Feeling coldness in our bodies,

But willing to feel the heat with a touch.

Both of us feeling drained,

Thinking where we go from here.

But I look through your watery eyes.

As you wrapped your arms around me,

And kiss your forehead.

I feel the warmth from your face.

I know it was worth the effort.

That I'll be forever,

By your side.

Fabiola Sully

Bullet-proof Heart

You fill your gun

With your shiny silver bullets.

You aim the gun

Right at my chest.

But you're sweating.

Afraid to pull the trigger,

Afraid you might kill me.

I'm not scared of you.

You can pull it all you want.

So go ahead,

Pull the goddamn trigger!

But remember this,

I'll be laughing in the end.

Fabiola Sully

My Way

For the timed I've been called crazy.

For the times I've been hurt.

For the times I've had dirt kicked in my face.

For the times I've been treated second class.

I look back on my past conquests.

I have some regrets; I have cried a few tears.

I even laid my heart on the line.

I fought battles I wasn't ready for.

And experience roadblocks and forks in my life.

But I was never ashamed.

Still I have been viewed as,

The lamb that strayed away from the pack.

Fabiola Sully

Whom wolves could have eaten

But still managed to find the way home.

I've been through hell and back.

But still have a smile on my face.

I never held anyone's hand.

Even if I was in need of one.

And through this ordeal

I have the scrapes and cuts to show it.

However, it doesn't bother me.

Cause I did it MY WAY!

Fabiola Sully

Untouchable

Every time I see you

You always seemed bothered.

You have something on your mind.

But you chose not to grow a smile

You give people dirty looks,

You carry a melancholy tune.

I see sadness in your eyes.

And the coldness in your stance.

Everybody steers away from you.

Feeling you will strike at anytime.

Giving out a roar

That fears anyone crossing your path.

I don't know how you're feeling.

Fabiola Sully

I just know you are in pain.

But you rather keep it inside.

And let it burn through your heart.

I've tried to show you love.

But it isn't sinking in.

I am afraid to even kiss you.

Knowing you'll give me frostbite.

You never see the tears

I have cried for you.

Or see how twisted,

I have become loving you.

I have to say good-by.

Because we will never be.

Sincerely, I label you…

Untouchable

Fabiola Sully

The Burden

Oh man,

You had to come to me.

You just had to come to me, huh.

I know your plan.

You gonna ruin my life.

You wanna see me suffer.

I've seen you do your damage.

To some friends of mine.

But you ain't gonna get me.

No way in hell.

I'm gonna get rid of you.

Fabiola Sully

I can't handle your pain.

But don't take it personally.

If I don't watch you bleed.

I can't handle your death.

Fabiola Sully

The Ride

You start out on a neutral level.

Then the fun begins.

Your throat's bone dry.

Your pulse is racing.

Your heart is pounding.

Faster and faster.

Louder and louder.

Not knowing where you are going.

Left or right.

No, up or down.

Just driving you up the wall.

Fabiola Sully

Now you are slowing down.

And all your energy is drained.

Thank you for hopping on.

And I'll see you very soon.

Fabiola Sully

Home

I've been traveling for days,

Trying to find my way home.

It feels like a never-ending journey

And I will never reach my point.

The days have been frying me.

And the nights leave me frozen.

I've even dealt with strong winds,

Blowing dirt and sand in my eyes.

I've been traveling for days,

Trying to find my way home.

I have walked many trails,

And the dirt roads along the way.

I seem to end up in dead ends

And detours along the way.

Fabiola Sully

I had to take different directions,

Which have left me confused.

I've been traveling for days,

Trying to find my way home.

The coyotes and vultures are always following me.

Waiting for my body to give in.

But one day I thought what's the use.

Until I saw home in my viewing.

It took all my strength,

And soul I had left to reach it.

I've been traveling for days,

Trying to find my way home.

The trip took a lot of me.

But I knew it was worth it.

Fabiola Sully

Strong Enough

Are you strong enough?

To be my man.

Can you handle me when I'm having my mood swings?

Or if I want to be by myself.

Can you handle me when I'm upset?

Or if I just want to talk.

Maybe you can handle loving me.

And quench my thirst and desires.

Can you handle me being different?

And understand my faults.

Now, are you strong enough?

Fabiola Sully

To be my man.

I am not saying I am a difficult person.

It just going to take a lot of time and patience,

Just to deal with me.

Fabiola Sully

Survival of the Fittest

Grab your weapons,

Roll out the tanks.

It's time to stand tall

And face the music

We've been taken the crap all our lives.

But not for long.

They have mocked us from time to time.

But all we do

Is sit on our rear ends.

And let it flow

Go after them,

Make them eat those words.

Show them what we are made of.

Show that we are not the wimps.

Fabiola Sully

They thought us to be.

We may get hurt.

We may even deal with their wicked ways.

But we ain't backing down.

We don't care if we are in pain.

Or if we die in battle.

But at least we have dignity.

On our side.

And they can't take that.

Away from us.

Fabiola Sully

Reality

You always have to look over your shoulder.

To know who's creeping behind you.

You always have to say I love myself.

When people say you're nothing.

You always have to deal with problems on your own

When nobody's around to help you.

You always have yourself to love.

When nobody loves you back

Dreams are good to have,

But this is what you have to deal with.

Fabiola Sully

Beyond this Feature

Beyond this feature

You'll see something special.

Something with beauty you can't imagine,

Something you've been searching for all your life.

Beyond this feature

Your true love lies.

I may be lead outside,

But I am pure gold inside.

Beyond this feature

Is something you were too blind to see.

Come a little closer

And see if you can open your eyes.

Fabiola Sully

Beyond this feature.

Is something none of them have.

It's a heart with love and laughter.

And all it needs is you.

Fabiola Sully

The Brick Wall

There's a brick wall

All around me

To keep me away from the poison.

And toxins from the other side.

Nobody could climb over it.

Or break it down,

The wall becomes bigger

And even stronger.

So I feel more secure.

Nobody could get to me.

But sometimes I feel

That the wall is laughing at me.

Fabiola Sully

It's Always the Quiet Ones

I'm a type of person,

Who sits in a room

And never says a word,

But you know what?

That's not the real me.

I'm louder than you think.

Fabiola Sully

To My Mother

I feel like I have betrayed you,

I feel have let you down,

I feel like I haven't done enough.

To show how much you mean to me.

You have done a lot for me,

You even broke your back

Trying to carry me,

Knowing I was a heavy load.

You took in so much

And you never said a word.

Even through you knew I was making mistakes

But watched me grow in the end.

I know I had some screw-ups.

I know I can be stubborn,

Fabiola Sully

But you knew I was finding myself,

And the woman I am supposed to be.

You tried to teach me about god.

And I thought he could never help me.

But judging by what you went through.

You have more strength and spirit than I do.

It's been hard for me to say,

Even through I have a lot on my mind.

You know I am here when you need me.

As you are for me.

www.ingramcontent.com/pod-product-compliance
Lightning Source LLC
Chambersburg PA
CBHW051448280526
45785CB00003B/1472